**PERSONAL FINANCE ON THE INTERNET,
AN INTERACTIVE GUIDE**

PERSONAL
Finance

Bernard J. WINGER
University of Dayton

Ralph R. FRASCA
University of Dayton

FIFTH EDITION

Prentice Hall
Upper Saddle River, New Jersey 07458

Acquisitions editor: *Paul Donnelly*
Associate editor: *Gladys Soto*
Project editor: *Theresa Festa*
Manufacturer: *Hamilton Printing Company, Lehigh Press*

©2000 by Prentice Hall, Inc.
Upper Saddle River, New Jersey 07458

All rights reserved. No part of this book may be
reproduced, in any form or by any means,
without permission in writing from the publisher.

Printed in the United States of America

10 9 8 7 6 5 4 3 2

ISBN 0-13-025546-7

Prentice-Hall International (UK) Limited, *London*
Prentice-Hall of Australia Pty. Limited, *Sydney*
Prentice-Hall Canada Inc., *Toronto*
Prentice-Hall Hispanoamericana, S.A., *Mexico*
Prentice-Hall of India Private Limited, *New Delhi*
Prentice-Hall of Japan, Inc., *Tokyo*
Prentice-Hall (Singapore) Pte Ltd
Editora Prentice-Hall do Brasil, Ltda., *Rio de Janeiro*

Table of Contents

Introduction iv
Chapter 1   Financial Planning: Why It's Important to You 1
Chapter 2   Financial Statements and Budgets: Where are You Now and Where are You Going? 3
Chapter 3   Cash Management: Funds for Immediate Needs 5
Chapter 4   Consumer Credit: Buying Now and Paying Later 7
Chapter 5   Taxes: The Government's Share of Your Rewards 10
Chapter 6   Life Insurance: Protecting Your Dependents 12
Chapter 7   Health Care and Disability Insurance: Protecting Your Earning Capacity ... 15
Chapter 8   Property and Liability Insurance: Protecting Your Lifestyle Assets 17
Chapter 9   Financial Markets and Institutions: Learning the Investment Environment ... 19
Chapter 10   Investment Basics: Understanding Risk and Return 21
Chapter 11   Common Stocks: Your Most Common Investment 23
Chapter 12   Fixed-Income Securities: An Important Alternative to Common Stocks ... 25
Chapter 13   Mutual Funds and Other Pooling Arrangements: Simplifying and Maybe Improving Your Investment Performance 27
Chapter 14   Other Investments: Expanding the Investment Menu 29
Chapter 15   Housing: The Cost of Shelter 31
Chapter 16   Consumer Durables: Satisfying Your Continuing Needs 34
Chapter 17   Retirement and Pension Planning: Planning for Your Long-Term Needs .. 37
Chapter 18   Estate Planning: Dividing up What's Left 40
Internet Addresses 41

Introduction

The Internet is a world wide information highway containing a multitude of resources on almost every imaginable topic. It is especially helpful for finding the latest news and information on financial topics which makes it particularly attractive in financial planning. A major drawback with the Internet is that it is too vast; unless you are selective, you will soon suffer from information overload. You will have more information than you can ever use.

These *Supplementary Internet Exercises* ease and direct your search with a list of sites that are integrated with topics covered in each chapter of the text. Each site is presented within the context of an exercise, which not only familiarizes you with Internet resources but also enhances your understanding of important personal finance concepts.

Personal finance must deal with real world concerns. Consequently, some of the links in these exercises are commercial sites. They are placed on the Net by businesses that want to sell you something. We do not recommend any of the goods and services advertised on the Internet, The sites were selected solely on the basis of their educational relevance. The businesses, of course, are providing the informational and programming content in an effort to gain your attention. Like other media, advertising is increasingly supporting the Internet.

We reviewed each of the links in the *Supplementary Internet Exercises* to confirm that all were operating at the date of publication. However, by the time you use them some may be outdated. As the links change we will update a hypertext version of this document that you can find at the author's website (**http://www.prenhall.com/winger**). By accessing this document or by downloading it to your own computer, you will save yourself the trouble of manually entering addresses. If you find that the links at our site are not functioning as intended, please let us know at *frasca@udayton.edu*. With your help we can kept this an up-to-date learning tool.

We were pleased to see the first edition of our exercises used by so many students of personal finance. Our own early experiences on the Internet indicated that it would be a significant aid to successful financial planning. Subsequent developments have proven us correct. However, the Internet's growth in speed, glitz, and information continues to amaze us. There is almost nothing you can't find on the Internet and almost no financial transaction you can't complete on the Internet. From shopping for life insurance to buying a home, the Internet can be an important source of information. But just like the shopper in a store, you should be wary of depending on information from individuals who profit off your expenditure. This is why surfing the electronic highway will never be a satisfactory substitute for a good course in personal finance and an impartial text.

From an educational perspective, there is no question that the biggest advantage of the Internet is that you can use it to continue your training *after* a course is finished, and for most college students that is when personal finance training will have its greatest impact. We feel strongly that the integration of text and Internet creates a learning environment offering life-long advantages; in a very real sense, your personal finance course can accompany you through your financial life

POINTERS ON ENTERING ADDRESSES

Bookmark Site

Your web browser should have an area where you can directly enter addresses (the official term is "uniform resource locator" or URL). Once you are at a site, you can probably bookmark it so that you may easily return to it again. Bookmaking a site is different for each browser. Consult the appropriate help file that accompanies your software.

Check Spelling and Capitalization

You must enter the address exactly as it appears in bold type at the bottom of each exercise. Capitalization is important, since some servers will interpret "Finance" as an entirely different word from "finance." If an address does not work, try retyping it to make sure you have correctly entered it. It is also possible that the addressed site no longer exists. Remember that we have a hypertext version of this document at **http://www.prenhall.com/winger**. If you want to avoid typing in addresses, then access our website directly.

Use a Search Engine

The Internet has a dynamic structure, with many new sites appearing and many old ones disappearing. Sometimes the site is still there, but the name of the file has changed. If this is the case, you may still be able to find the resource by using one of the search engines on the Net.

Search engines allow you to enter a word, a combination of key words, or a phrase. The engine then searches for pages on the Internet that best fit what you are looking for. Some sources provide a compilation of search engines, making it easy for you to try out several search engines if your first choice proves unsatisfactory. Both of the major browsers have direct links to search engines that you can be use to find other search engines.

After a while, you will probably find one search engine that satisfies your needs and is more comfortable to use than the others. Whichever search engine you choose, be sure to review any available hints on searching. Each search engine is likely to have some special rules for entering search terms that can significantly increase your ability to find what you are seeking.

Chapter 1
FINANCIAL PLANNING
Why It's Important to You

WHY STUDY PERSONAL FINANCE?

Exercise 1.1 Finding Your Personal Goals

Determining your personal and financial goals may be a difficult task. You might want to begin by examining your personal value system, using the questionnaire developed by the Values and Lifestyles Program (VALS) at SRI.

Q. Answer the survey questions and find your primary and secondary types. Click on the types for their explanations, then explain how your types might influence your approach to financial planning.

A.

Exercise 1.2 Following the Economy

Keep up with current economic events by using the Bureau of Labor Statistics data and choosing the series of interest to you. Click on the graphic for a graph of the series, which gives the information more effectively than the tables. For the question below, choose the "Unemployment Rate" series.

Q. What has been the highest unemployment rate since 1989? Suppose the unemployment rate is 10% at the time you graduate. What implication might such a rate have with respect to your job-search efforts?

A.

ACHIEVING GOALS THROUGH PLANNING

Exercise 1.3 An Overview of Financial Calculators

Financial calculations involving the time value of money are an important part of financial planning. These calculations are difficult, but there are many helpful computational engines available on the Internet. Most of these are dedicated to performing specific tasks. To review some, see Martindale's 'The Reference Desk' or conduct a Yahoo Search.

Exercise 1.4 Finding the Future Value of a Single Payment and an Annuity

Several of the calculators can be used for time value problems in general. For example, go to Centura Money Managers. Click on "How fast will my money grow?" to answer the first question and "How much faster will my money grow?" to answer the second.

Q. You hope to receive $5,000 in graduation gifts, which you will invest for your retirement in 30 years. If you can earn 12% each year, how much will you have in the retirement fund at the end of 30 years?

A.

Q. You want to buy a $20,000 car in 3 years. If you can invest $6,300 a year and earn 8% each year, will you have enough funds at the end of three years?

A.

Exercise 1.5 Finding the Present Value of a Single Payment

Money received in the future has less value than money available today. Money Advisor has a calculator that finds the discounted value of a future payment.

Q. Assume today's date is 01/01/99 and you will receive a gift of $1,000 on 01/01/05. If the discount rate is 10 percent, what is the present value?

A.

Chapter 2
FINANCIAL STATEMENTS AND BUDGETS
Where are You Now and Where are You Going?

INCOME STATEMENTS

Exercise 2.1 What is Your Spending Personality?

Your spending personality assessment may be revealed by answering a questionnaire from HealthyCash.

Q. What are your buying habits? Explain if you may have shopping problems that can hinder your saving effort.

A.

EVALUATING FINANCIAL PERFORMANCE

Exercise 2.2 Is Your Income Matching the Inflation Rate?

Find the most recent inflation rate by consulting Economic Statistics Briefing Room. Scroll down and choose Prices.

Q. How much must your income increase each year to match the most recent inflation rate?

A.

ACHIEVING GOALS THROUGH BUDGETING

Exercise 2.3 Setting Up a Budget

Along with the text's treatment, some additional help in setting up a budget is provided by Household Budget Management. Choose "What is a Household Budget." Then, scroll down and choose "A Sample Budget."

Q. Compare their budget to the one in Chapter 2.

A.

Exercise 2.4 How Do Other People Spend Their Money?

The BLS Consumer Expenditure Survey shows expenditures for the average American family. The Steeles spent 28% of their income on housing.

Q. What percentage does the average family spend on housing? Suppose your rent is 40% of your income. What problems can this create in your effort to balance your budget?

A.

Exercise 2.5 Do You Have a Typical Budget?

Money Online has a budget maker that allows you to enter your personal data and then analyze your spending.

Q. After entering appropriate data, how does your spending compare to other people like you?

A.

Chapter 3
CASH MANAGEMENT
Funds for Immediate Needs

MEETING CASH NEEDS

Exercise 3.1 How Can You Join a Credit Union?

If your employer does not have a credit union, you still may have an opportunity to join one. Consult CUNA & Affiliates and answer the following question.

Q. What are the six ways to join a credit union?

A.

Exercise 3.2 Where Can You Earn the Highest Returns on Your Cash Deposits?

USA Today helps you find financial institutions offering the highest yields on bank deposits, money market funds, and Treasury securities.

Q. Suppose you are helping your parents invest $80,000 over the next 6 months. Where can you get the highest return? Is it with a 6-month CD or 6-month Treasury bill? If it's a CD, find the phone number of the offering institution, then call to determine if the account has federal insurance.

A.

Exercise 3.3 What is the Trend in Short-Term Interest Rates?

Interest rates are often volatile over time. The Economics Time Series Page at the University of Alabama provides data and charts on over 75,000 series. You can use this sit to examine the trend in financial data. Browse the interest rate data at the Federal Reserve, Board of Governors.

Q. What is the current trend in the 1-Year Treasury Bill Rate (Auction Average)?

A.

Q. How doe this rate on 1-Year Treasury Bills compare with the Bank Prime Loan Rate?

A.

USING YOUR CHECKING ACCOUNT

Exercise 3.4 Can I Pay Bills over the Internet—and How Much Does It Cost?

You can use the Internet to pay bills. See what Checkfree Corporation and Network Payment Mechanisms have to offer.

Q. See if your financial institution offers online banking by choosing "Electronic Commerce - Consumers."

A.

UNDERSTANDING HOW YOUR ACCOUNT EARNS INTEREST

Example 3.5 Finding Nominal and Effective Yields

What is the effective yield on an account that compounds more frequently than once a year? Consult Money Advisor, go to "Loans and Savings Calculators," and click on "Nominal and Effective Interest Rates."

Q. Enter: 3425.94 for future value, 1000 for present value, 16 for years, and 1 for compounding frequency. What are the nominal and effective rates? Now enter 3596.13 for future value, 1000 for present value, 16 for years, and 365 for compounding frequency. What are the nominal and effective rates? Compare your answers.

A.

Chapter 4
CONSUMER CREDIT
Buying Now and Paying Later

ARRANGING AND USING CREDIT

Exercise 4.1 Obtain a Credit Report
You can link to Trans Union, TRW (Experian), and Equifax for information on obtaining your credit report.

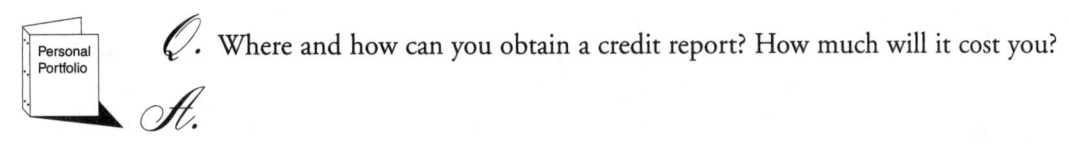

Q. Where and how can you obtain a credit report? How much will it cost you?

A.

SALES CREDIT

Exercise 4.2 Comparing Credit Card Offers
The Bank Rate Monitor provides information on numerous credit card offers. For each the terms and conditions are listed. Select two of the offers and compare the terms and conditions.

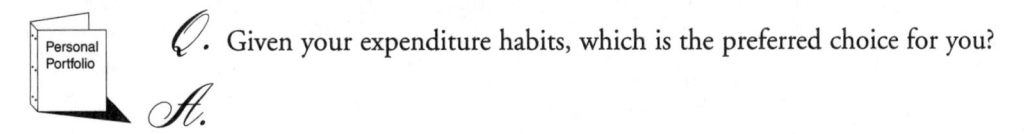

Q. Given your expenditure habits, which is the preferred choice for you?

A.

Exercise 4.3 Should You Prepay a Loan?
This utilizes another one of the great financial calculators from Hugh Chou. The Prepayment vs. Investment Calculator determines when it is beneficial to make early payments on a mortgage. However, the results can be extended to any installment type loan with simple interest payments.

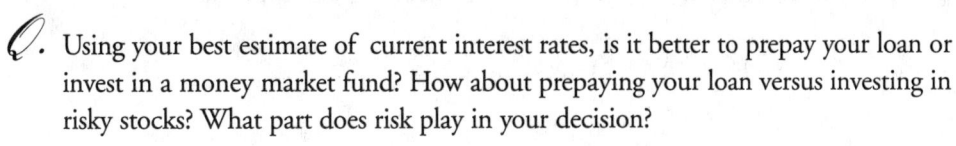

Q. Using your best estimate of current interest rates, is it better to prepay your loan or invest in a money market fund? How about prepaying your loan versus investing in risky stocks? What part does risk play in your decision?

A.

CASH CREDIT

Exercise 4.4 How the Interest Rate Affects Your Debt Repayments

The interest rate can significantly influence the size and term of your debt repayments. This can be illustrated with the aid of several financial calculators on the Internet. The most appropriate one for this project is the Unknown Loan Variables Calculator from Bank 2000. Assuming compounding with simple interest, this program can calculate the number of periods needed to pay off a loan given the monthly dollar payments. You can also calculate the monthly dollar payment needed to pay off a loan in a given number of installments.

Calculate the monthly payment on a 24-month installment loan of $5,000 at both an 18% annual rate of interest and a 15% annual rate of interest.

Q. At the lower interest rate, how much do you save on monthly payments and total interest payments?

A.

Calculate how long it would take to pay off a $5,000 loan balance with monthly payments of $100 at both an 18% and 15% annual rate of interest.

Q. How much longer does it take to pay off the loan at the higher interest rate, and how much more do you pay in total interest payments?

A.

OBTAINING CREDIT AND RESOLVING CREDIT PROBLEMS

Exercise 4.5 Interest Rate Comparisons

Using the Bank Rate Monitor Home Equity Loan Page, find the lowest rate on a home equity loan in the closest geographic market. Compare this with the lowest rate on a credit card in the same geographic market from the Bank Rate Monitor Credit Card Home Page.

Q. Which is the better deal?

A.

Exercise 4.6 Changes in Interest Rates

The Federal Reserve Bank publishes data on the types of loans listed in Figure 4.8. These are placed on the Internet at the St. Louis Federal Reserve Bank. The Federal Reserve Bank Database (FRED) contains data on most financial series. Compare data on the most recent rates with those listed in Figure 4.8.

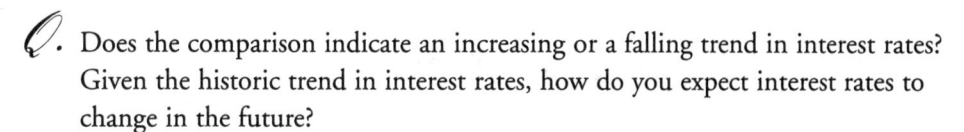

Q. Does the comparison indicate an increasing or a falling trend in interest rates? Given the historic trend in interest rates, how do you expect interest rates to change in the future?

A.

Exercise 4.7 The Card You Pick Can Save You Money

Every six months the Federal Reserve System collects data on credit cards offered by major financial institutions. The data are published in a bulletin and on the Internet under the title "The Card You Pick Can Save You Money." The survey reveals a variety of offers over a wide range of interest rates and annual fees.

Q. What are the highest and lowest interest rates in the latest survey? What are the highest and lowest annual fees in the latest survey?

A.

Chapter 5
TAXES
The Government's Share of Your Rewards

DETERMINING YOUR FEDERAL INCOME TAXES

Exercise 5.1 Keeping Up with Changes in the Tax Code

Each year Congress makes at least minor changes in the tax code. Those people who are aware of the changes can often modify their personal financial plans so that the changes work in their favor. Deloitte & Touche OnLine, a web site provided by the accounting firm of the same name, highlights recent changes in the law that affect individuals.

Q. How might recent changes in the tax law influence your current or future financial decisions?

A.

OTHER ASPECTS OF FEDERAL INCOME TAX

Exercise 5.2 What's an Enrolled Agent (EA)?

If you are audited by the IRS, an Enrolled Agent can appear at the Internal Revenue Service in your place. How do you locate an Enrolled Agent? The answer to this and other questions concerning Enrolled Agents appear at the web site for the National Association of Enrolled Agents.

Q. How does one become an EA, and what are the entry requirements for this profession?

A.

Exercise 5.3 Are You Audit Bait?

Want to know how to avoid being audited or whether you are likely to be audited? This site by Online Money will give you the answers.

Q. What actions can increase your chances of an audit?

A.

OTHER IMPORTANT TAXES

Exercise 5.4 Locating Information on State Taxes

The Internal Revenue Service provides tax forms, informational publications, and tax tips. Determine what type of information is available from your state government. In your hunt, you can use a general search program link at Cnet Central, or you can use one of the special pages with state government links. For example, try Federal Tax Administrators or the Tax Sites State Government Tax List.

Q. Can you electronically access information on your state taxes? If so, at what site?

A.

Exercise 5.5 Determining the Top State Marginal Tax Rate.

Most states tax income in a manner consistent with the federal government's taxation of income. If your state has an income tax, what is its top marginal tax rate and at what level of taxable income does this rate become effective? What state has the top marginal tax rate in the nation? This information is available from the Federation of Tax Administrators, an association of major state-tax collection agencies.

Q. If your state has an income tax, what is the top marginal rate in your state, and at what level of taxable income does this rate become effective?

A.

Chapter 6
LIFE INSURANCE
Protecting Your Dependents

ESTIMATING YOUR LIFE INSURANCE NEEDS

Exercise 6.1 Calculating Your Worth

The Life and Health Insurance Foundation for Education provides several different calculators for estimating insurance needs. The calculator for Human Life Value Analysis calculates the amount needed in the family maintenance fund to replace a given percentage of your income from your current age through your date of expected retirement. The present value of the investment fund is based upon an assumed interest rate, inflation rate and tax rate. Initial values are entered by the program, but you may change these if your wish.

Enter the following information: Assume an annual income of $30,000 and personal maintenance expenses at 30% of your annual income. Choose values for the other variables that you think are appropriate.

Q. Given these assumptions what is the net present value of the lost support to your family?

A.

Exercise 6.2 Calculating Your Insurance Needs

The Life and Health Insurance Foundation for Education also provides an Insurance Needs Calculator. You begin by entering the cash needs at death, the mortgage payoff, and anticipated college funding. To this amount it adds the present value of maintenance for the surviving spouse less current investments and existing life insurance.

Enter the amounts you think are appropriate for a married couple with two children and a 30 year-old head of household.

Q. If this family does not have any life insurance, what is the Life Insurance Protection Gap?

A.

Exercise 6.3 Obtaining an Estimate of Social Security Benefits

Want to know how much your survivors will receive in Social Security benefits? You can electronically request a copy of your Personal Earnings and Benefit Estimate Statement at Social Security Online. In the future you will receive an immediate response on your computer. For now, however, you have to wait for the snail mail to deliver your statement.

Q. Review your Personal Earnings and Benefit Estimate Statement. Are your historic wages accurately listed on this form? If you don't have your own statement, you can review the sample statement at Social Security Online.

A.

Exercise 6.4 What is Your Probability of Survival?

Life tables, like those included in the Social Security Statistical Tables published by the Social Security Administration, can provide estimates on your probability of survival. For a given age group they predict how many individuals are likely to survive to subsequent ages.

Q. Look at the life table. For an individual of your age and gender, what is your probability of survival over the next year? What is your probability of survival over the next ten years? Hint: Given 100,000 males born alive, if 97,491 are alive at age 25 and 95,777 are alive at age 35, then the probability of surviving from age 25 to age 35 is .982 = (95,777 / 97,491).

A.

Exercise 6.5 Playing the Longevity Game

How long can you expect to live? Northwestern Mutual Life's online life expectancy calculator factors in genetic and lifestyle characteristics to estimate your life expectancy. The probabilities of survival are based on data gathered by private life insurance companies and public agencies. Remember, you are calculating an average. This means that half the population with similar characteristics is expected to exceed this life expectancy and half is not.

Q. Enter you own characteristics. What is your life expectancy? Change one of the lifestyle characteristics you have control over. How does this change your life expectancy?

A.

SELECTING THE RIGHT POLICY

Exercise 6.6 Pricing Term Insurance

There are numerous sites on the web that will provide a price quote on term insurance. Most, however, require that you be willing to provide the insurance company with some personal information. Commercial Union Life lets you instantaneously obtain a sample price on term insurance without the hassle. This can provide you with some insight on how the cost of term insurance may vary with your personal characteristics. Other useful quote sites are QuickQuote, KeyPartners, Quotesmith, and IntelliQuote.

Price a $100,000 5-year term policy for yourself at age 25 and at age 45.

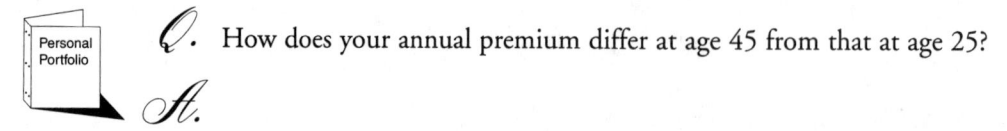

Q. How does your annual premium differ at age 45 from that at age 25?

A.

Exercise 6.7 Checking the Ratings on Insurance Companies

The Insurance News Network provides financial ratings on an extensive list of life and health insurance companies. The ratings are determined by both Standard & Poors Corp. and Duff & Phelps Credit Rating.

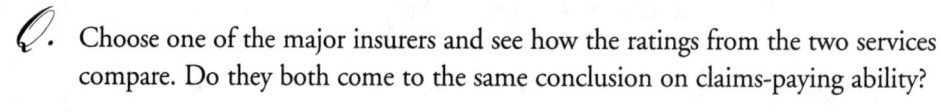

Q. Choose one of the major insurers and see how the ratings from the two services compare. Do they both come to the same conclusion on claims-paying ability?

A.

Chapter 7
HEALTH CARE AND DISABILITY INSURANCE
Protecting Your Earning Capacity

HEALTH CARE INSURANCE

Exercise 7.1 Comparison Shopping for Health Care Plans

Test your ability to evaluate health insurance policies at the California Health Care Shopper. Here you will find a list of HMOs, PPOs, and POSs in California. Full plan descriptions are provided along with monthly fees.

Personal Portfolio

Q. Select an HMO and a PPO, and determine which one provides the better basic health care coverage and which one provides the preferred major medical coverage. Which is the better plan for you? Why?

A.

Exercise 7.2 Obtaining Comparative Data on Hospitals

QuadroMed Corporation has created the American Hospital Directory. It is a database of information on hospitals. The raw data were collected by the government. QuadroMed created a convenient online database for accessing this information. It provides a free service and a subscription service for using this database. The free service provides only summary data. However, this is probably sufficient information for most consumers. You can also search a database at the Joint Commission on Accreditation of Healthcare Organizations to review your hospital's accreditation status.

Q. Check on a hospital in your area. What is the average length of stay in this hospital? Is it accredited by some reviewing agency?

A.

Exercise 7.3 Review a Living Will

Rio Grande Free-Net serves up a Healthcare Guide to medical care resources on the web. If you dig down through the menus, you will find a page on Advanced Directives. Consider whether this document reflects your own wishes. An alternative living will can be found at the Consumer Guide to Advance Directives from the Group Health Cooperative of Puget Sound.

Q. What would you put in an advanced directive that reflects your own wishes?

A.

Exercise 7.4 Get a Report Card on Your Local Managed Care Plans

The National Committee on Quality Assurance has derived a system called HEDIS for rating managed care providers. It accredits those health care plans that meet its standards. Find out about the accreditation standards and determine whether the managed care plans in your area are accredited at this website. You can search the data base or download the entire list of accredited plans.

Q. Select a managed care plan in your area. Is this an accredited plan?

A.

DISABILITY INCOME PROTECTION

Exercise 7.5 Obtaining an Estimate of Social Security Disability Benefits

If you didn't obtain a copy of your Social Security benefits in the previous chapter, you can do it now to determine your disability benefits. You can now obtain an estimate of your Personal Earnings and Benefit Estimate Statement from Social Security Online . You will receive a reply to your electronic request by snail mail.

Q. What are your estimated monthly disability benefits? If you don't have your own statement, you can review the sample statement at Social Security Online.

A.

Chapter 8
PROPERTY AND LIABILITY INSURANCE
Protecting Your Lifestyle Assets

HOMEOWNERS' INSURANCE

Exercise 8.1 Check the Financial Stability of Property Casualty Insurers

In the event of a major catastrophe, like hurricane Hugo, property casualty insurers must have adequate reserves to cover the liabilities. The Insurance News Network provides Standard and Poors ratings of property/casualty insurers and life/health insurers.

Q. Choose a company with a triple A rating and one that has a triple B rating. Determine why these companies are rated differently.

A.

Exercise 8.2 Find the Average Cost of Homeowner's Insurance

The Insurance News Network provides information on the average cost of homeowner's insurance by state. Go to the state link for your additional information.

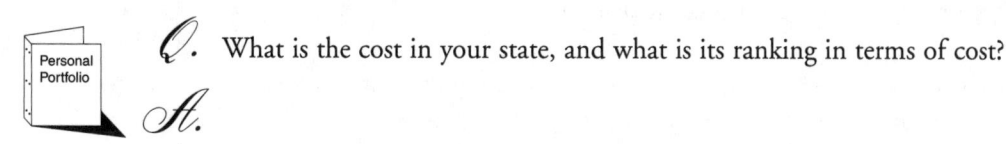

Q. What is the cost in your state, and what is its ranking in terms of cost?

A.

AUTOMOBILE INSURANCE

Exercise 8.3 What are the Minimum Liability Limits in Your State?

Each state requires car owners to purchase a minimum amount of auto liability coverage. This minimum amount is probably less than you should have. However, this may be what the other driver on the road has. Consequently, you should be aware of your state's minimum. This information can also be found at the Insurance News Network on a page entitled "Minimum levels of required auto liability insurance." The minimums are listed in terms of split liability coverage.

Q. What is the minimum split liability coverage in your state? Explain how the split liability limit is applied to bodily injury and property damage.

A.

Exercise 8.4 What is the Cost of Auto Insurance?

The Insurance Information News Gateway to State Insurance Information has the average cost of auto insurance by state and be type of insurance. Check out the cost in your state. For the states listed in bold on this page there are average premiums for regions or cities within the state.

Q. What is the average cost of auto insurance in your state, and what is the legal minimum on liability coverage?

A.

Exercise 8.5 Will Your Car be Stolen?

If thieves like your car, you will probably have to pay a high premium for coverage against theft. The Highway Loss Data Institute collects data on this and other factors that affect auto insurance premiums. This information is published on the Web by the Insurance News Network. Review the Relative Average Loss Payment Per Insured Vehicle.

Q. How does the loss rating for your or your family's auto compare to that of the average auto? If your model year is not listed, use the closest model and year.

A.

Exercise 8.6 Driver Death Rates

The Highway Loss Data Institute publishes driver death rates by make and model of car, which takes into account the crash worthiness of the vehicle and the characteristics of individuals that drive a certain type of vehicle. Vehicles with higher death rates are likely to have higher insurance premiums.

Q. Check out the Death Rates by Make and Model for the car you own or usually ride in. How does this car compare with the average vehicle in its class?

A.

Chapter 9
FINANCIAL MARKETS AND INSTITUTIONS
Learning the Investment Environment

GOALS AND INVESTMENT ALTERNATIVES

Exercise 9.1 What Are Your Investment Goals and What Is Your Comfort Zone?

Before investing, you should review your overall financial goals. Help is provided by Prudential Securities. Click on "Life's Financial Concerns" for a good discussion of the importance of establishing goals. Then click on the "Personality Quiz" to determine your investment personality.

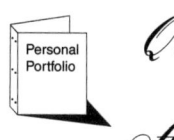

Personal Portfolio

Q. What is your quiz score and what is your "comfort zone"? Based on these outcomes, what type of investor are you likely to be?

A.

SECURITIES MARKETS

Exercise 9.2 How Does the NYSE Differ from the OTC Market?

The New York Stock Exchange has a useful site. Click on "The NYSE" for a menu of topics. Then click the "Auction Market."

Q. How does the NYSE differ from the over-the-counter market?

A.

Exercise 9.3 What's Happening to NASDAQ?

NASDAQ maintains a lively market page that tracks trading activity during the day.

Q. Compare the NASDAQ Index to the DJIA. Are they moving in the same direction?

A.

REGULATION OF THE SECURITIES INDUSTRY

Exercise 9.4 Advice from the SEC

An important source of securities regulation is the Securities and Exchange Commission (SEC) Visit its site for considerable information, beginning with "Investor Assistance and Complaints." Then scroll down and click on "Invest Wisely."

Q. What telephone number can you call to determine if any brokerage firm or sales representative has a disciplinary history?

A.

USING THE SERVICES OF A STOCKBROKER

Exercise 9.5 Planning for a Child's College Education

Most full-service brokers, such as Smith/Barney, have Internet sites that offer a variety of services. Take a look at its "Financial Planning" for a good presentation of planning for future goals. Click on "Funding Your Child's Education."

Q. What has been the annual inflation rate of the average cost of a four-year university education over the past twenty years?

A.

Exercise 9.6 Trading Over the Internet

Some firms specialize in internet trading. See what E-Trade offers . Click on "Open An Account."

Q. What is the minimum investment amount needed to open a margin account?

A.

Chapter 10
INVESTMENT BASICS
Understanding Risk and Return

RISK AND RETURN

Exercise 10.1 Compare Risk and the Holding Period Length

The Vanguard family of mutual funds provides helpful investment information in many areas. Click on "Plain Talk about Realistic Expectations."

Q. Is the range of stock returns greater for 1-year holding periods or 25-year holding periods? What implication does the answer have in terms of how frequently assets should be bought and sold? Relate this last answer to the discussion of risk and time in the text.

A.

Exercise 10.2 What's the Market Doing?

There are many excellent Internet sites providing information on individual securities and the markets overall. One of the best is Security APL, Inc. Click on "Market Watch" to review the performances of the popular indexes throughout the day. Then click on "Standard and Poors" to view the day's graphic of this index. Scrolling down the page, you can find performance graphics for other periods of time.

Q. What has been the highest value for the S&P 500 over the past 10 years?

A.

APPLYING A RISK-RETURN MODEL

Exercise 10.3 What's Intel Doing?

While at Security APL's site, find out what Intel is doing by entering its symbol (INTC) in the block (first, click on the block). Along with the most recent price, other information appears. For even more information on Intel, go to WSRN.com and enter Intel's symbol. Under the Graphs and Charts heading choose "Quick Source: Description and Stats."

Q. What is Intel's beta and its 5-year EPS growth rate?

A.

BUILDING AND CHANGING A PORTFOLIO

Exercise 10.4 Does P&G Have a Dividend Reinvestment Program (DRIP)?

DRIPS are very popular. You can find a list of companies with dividend reinvestment programs at the Netstock Direct site. Go to the site and click the "Search" hyperlink.

Q. Does P&G (PG) have a DRIP?

A.

Exercise 10.5 How Does Dollar Cost Averaging (DCA) Work?

DCA is a popular investment strategy that avoids the perils of "playing the market."

Q. Review the example provided by Regatta Q on its page Retire in Style. How many shares did Dianne purchase during the year with DCA? How many would she have purchased by investing the full amount on January 1?

A.

Chapter 11
COMMON STOCKS
Your Most Common Investment

CHARACTERISTICS OF COMMON STOCKS

Exercise 11.1 How Are the Dogs of the Dow Doing?

Many investors rely upon a company's dividend yield as a guide for selecting companies. Read about a popular approach called Dogs of the Dow (page 284 of the text provides background). Click on "Performance" to compare the approach to the overall Dow Jones Industrial Average.

Q. For the current year, are the Dogs of the Dow beating the overall market?

A.

FUNDAMENTAL ANALYSIS OF COMMON STOCKS

Exercise 11.2 How Is Mead Doing?

There are a number of excellent sites providing both quotes and company data. We noted the Security APL, Inc. site above. Now try Yahoo Quotes. Enter Mead's symbol, MEA, in the request block and receive the price quote. Click on "Company News" to see if any news items occurred recently. Choose "Charts" to get a great price chart. Choose "Research" to find recommendations on securities analysts.

Another great source of information is DBC Online. Enter MEA at the symbol request. Along with the quote, you get a great price chart. Under "Select Option" choose "Data" and then click on "Submit." A variety of information emerges.

Q. What is Mead's average recommendation?

A.

Exercise 11.3 What Are Mead's Most Current Quarterly Earnings?

If you really want volumes of a company's data, go directly to the forms it must file with the Securities and Exchange Commission (SEC). Scroll down to "Enter a Company" and enter Mead. Click on "Submit Choice" and see all reports filed by Mead. Choose the 10Q report, which is a company's quarterly report. Choose the 10Q dated 08-07-1996 and look for the Statement of Earnings.

Q. What were Mead's earnings per share (EPS) in that quarter?

A.

TECHNICAL ANALYSIS

Exercise 11.4 What Does Mead's Chart Look Like?

For a quick quote and an accompanying chart, see Stockmaster and enter Mead's symbol MEA.

Q. Does it appear that Mead is outperforming the S&P500?

A.

Exercise 11.5 What's the A/D Line Doing?

Technical analysts follow many so-called pressure indicators, such as the Advance/Decline Line illustrated at DecisionPoint.Com.

Q. Select DecisionPoint's "Current Chart." Is the A/D Line and the NYSE Composite moving in the same direction?

A.

Chapter 12
FIXED-INCOME SECURITIES
An Important Alternative to Common Stocks

CORPORATE-ISSUED BONDS

Exercise 12.1 Help for the Bond Investor

You can find information about all kinds of bonds—corporates, Treasuries, and municipals—with Bonds On-Line. An attractive feature of this site is the Bond Professor, which answers questions about bonds. Another attractive feature is found by choosing "Corporates" and then "Corporate Bond Search." Find the answer to the following question, choosing "Corporates."

Q. Suppose you want a bond with a maturity between 10 and 20 years and a coupon rate of 6 to 10 percent. Enter these data. What list of corporate bonds does the search suggest?

A.

GOVERNMENT-ISSUED BONDS

Exercise 12.2 How Can I Buy Treasuries without Paying a Broker's Commission?

The Federal Reserve Bank of New York provides information on buying Treasury bonds. At the home page, click on "Treasury Direct" for information and forms.

Q. How can you buy Treasury bonds without paying a broker's commission? What procedures must you follow?

A.

Exercise 12.3 What Are My Savings Bonds Worth Right Now?

Stay at the above Federal Reserve site, go back to the home page, and click on "Savings Bonds." Now click on "Redemption Calculator" and find the series that you own. You can also download the "Savings Bond Wizard," a free program that helps you manage your savings bonds.

Q. Use the Redemption Calculator. What is the redemption value for a savings bond from issue date January 1995 to issue date Jan 1999? Choose $25 face value ($12.50 investment).

A.

Exercise 12.4 What Are the Closing Prices of Some Treasury Bonds?

The Fed no longer provides closing prices on Treasury Bonds. Selected prices, however, can be found at CBS MarketWatch. Choose "Market Data," then "Treasuries." The selected maturities provide an overview of the yield curve.

Q. What is the closing price on the five-year treasury. What is the coupon rate on this bond and the date of maturity? Refer to the text on how to convert this quote to dollars and cents.

A.

Chapter 13
MUTUAL FUNDS AND OTHER POOLING ARRANGEMENTS
Simplifying and Maybe Improving Your Investment Performance

MUTUAL FUNDS

Exercise 13.1 Does Fidelity Have a Growth Fund?

Many mutual fund families, such as Vanguard's, have web sites. For another great site, visit the Fidelity Investment Center. Click on "Mutual Funds" and then click on "Fidelity Funds" for comprehensive information, including performance measurements, on any Fidelity fund. Funds are grouped by objective, and you must choose a fund through this criterion. For example, choosing "growth," you get a list of the specific funds that are growth oriented. Click on the fund that interests you.

Q. How many growth funds does Fidelity offer?

A.

Exercise 13.2 What Are Closed-End Funds?

Closed-end funds offer certain advantages and disadvantages in relation to open-end funds. Go to Essential Information on mutual funds at the ICI site and review A Guide to Closed End Funds.

Q. How many closed-end funds are there? Are bond funds more numerous than stock (equity) funds?

A.

Exercise 13.3 How Many Stars Does the Berger 100 Fund Have?

A premier mutual fund evaluation service is Morningstar, which also provides a web site Morningstar Fund Reports. You can browse the alphabetical index at no charge and find the Morningstar rating for many funds.

Q. What's the rating for the Berger 100 Fund? Click on "B" and keep scrolling until you find the fund.

A.

Exercise 13.4 Ask Mutual Fund Experts

A useful site for mutual fund investors is Mutual Funds Interactive. You can find considerable data for funds, including price charts. Clicking on "Expert's Corner" gives you insights and advice from mutual fund professionals.

INVESTMENT TRUSTS

Exercise 13.5 Where Can You Find a High-Performing REIT?

The National Association of Real Estate Investment Trusts can help answer this question and also provide much more information about REITs. At the home page, click on "Research and Statistics," then "REIT Database."

Q. How many REITs had an annual return of 30% or more over the past 12 months? (Click on "ALL" in each information box.)

A.

LIMITED PARTNERSHIPS AND INVESTMENT CLUBS

Exercise 13.6 Want to Join an Investment Club?

If your answer is "yes," or if you simply want to learn more about investment clubs, or if you want to find some sound ideas on investing in general, visit the National Association of Investment Clubs site.

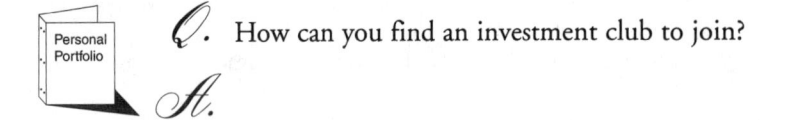

Q. How can you find an investment club to join?

A.

Chapter 14
OTHER INVESTMENTS
Expanding the Investment Menu

REAL ESTATE

Exercise 14.1 Are the Housing Demographics Changing?

Population demographics are the underpinning of housing demand. The Census Bureau provides sample data to help you review population and housing trends.

Q. How many occupied housing units were counted in the last census? What percent were owner-occupied?

A.

Exercise 14.2 Want to Buy or Rent a Time Share?

The Time Share Users Group has a web site dedicated to time shares. Click on "Classified Ads" for information.

Q. What are the top ten resorts?

A.

OTHER TANGIBLE ASSETS

Exercise 14.3 What's the Price on the Double Eagle?

The American Numismatic Association has information on collections of coin and currency. However, if you want a price on a Double Eagle you will have to visit one of the dealers. The American Gold Coin site can help answer this question and others regarding the value of gold coins. Click on "Double Eagle." Prices depend upon condition, so review the definitions of condition carefully.

Q. What's the price of a mint-condition Double Eagle?

A.

Exercise 14.4 What's the 5-Year Return on the American Century Gold Fund?

EagleWing Research provides information on gold funds. Click on "38 U.S. Gold Funds" for data on 38 funds and useful links to other sites. Click on N2 in the row for the American Century fund and examine the graphic.

Q. What is the 5-year return on the American Century Global Gold Fund?

A.

DERIVATIVE SECURITIES

Exercise 14.5 What's Corn Doing?

The Chicago Board of Trade has a great site—one worth visiting even if you never trade a commodity futures contract. Review all the information available at the home page. Then click on "Market Plex Quotes," then "Quotes and Data," then "10-Minute Delayed Futures Quotes," and finally "Day" in the Corn listing, which appears in the column labeled Day Session. You will find a variety of price quotes related to different contract maturities. Divide the quotes by 1000 to read the actual price.

Q. What is the current price of corn, and how does this price compare to the one in Table 14.6 of the text?

A.

Exercise 14.6 Should Beanie Babies Be Part of Your Portfolio?

Ty Company has done a superb job of marketing its sole product - Beanie Babies. Part of the marketing plan is to periodically retire some Babies.

Q. Go to The Best Price Guide to see market prices on retired Beanie Babies. How much have the retired Babies appreciated?

A.

Chapter 15
HOUSING
The Cost of Shelter

RENT OR BUY?

Exercise 15.1 How Much House Can You Afford?

The Finance Center has several calculators to help you with your housing decision. Two that fit nicely into the discussion in the text are the "How Much Can I Borrow?" worksheet and the "Am I Better Off Renting?" worksheet. The mortgage worksheet gives you a range of possible outcomes based on how much you are willing to put down and your lender's attitude toward risk.

Q. Given the sample data, enter a 20 percent down payment and vary the interest rate from 6% to 9%. How does the affordable home price change as the interest rate changes?

A.

Exercise 15.2 Rent or Buy?

Return to the Finance Center website and click on the worksheet, Am I Better Off Renting? The graph on the rent/buy worksheet is a real plus. With one glance you can observe the year in which the cost of renting begins to exceed the cost of buying. As we state in the text, buying is likely to be the preferred alternative the longer you plan to stay in one place. With this worksheet graph, you can easily determine the point of indifference between buying and renting.

Q. Use the sample data in the Am I Better Off Renting? worksheet, but vary the appreci-ation rate on homes from 3 to 5 percent. Also, vary the interest rate on the mort-gage from 7 to 9 percent. How do these changes affect the decision to buy or rent? How many years would you have to live at the same location for you to be financially indifferent to buying versus selling?

A.

Exercise 15.3 Evaluating the Neighborhood

The market value of a home depends on more than just the number of rooms. To a large extent, the price of a home depends on the community it is located in. Coldwell Banker has a nationwide chain of real estate firms. In addition to providing online listings of homes, it also provides summary data on neighborhoods to help you evaluate the community. You can access this information through its Neighborhood Explorer (TM).

More difficult to use, but with much more detailed data, is the TIGER Map Service from the U.S. Census.

Both sites permit you to obtain socioeconomic data by zipcode. They are most helpful when comparing neighborhoods within a city. You can try them out by comparing your own neighborhood with some other well-known community.

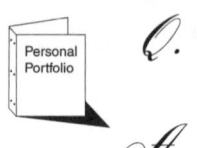

Q. Using either of these online sites, compare the socioeconomic data on your own neighborhood with that from zipcode 90210, the famous Beverly Hills community.

A.

FINANCING THE PURCHASE

Exercise 15.4 Generate an Amortization Table

The Mortgage Calculator from Mortgage Market Information Services generates an amortization table indicating the remaining balance on your loan after each mortgage payment. It also indicates how much you must increase your monthly payment for you to pay off the mortgage at an earlier date. A $100,000 30-year mortgage at 7.5% APR would require monthly payments of $699.21.

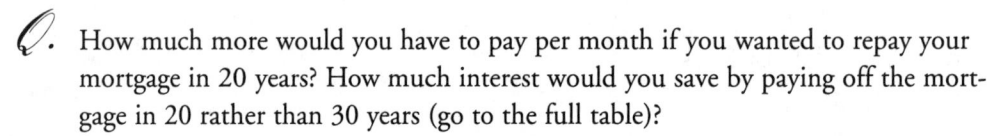

Q. How much more would you have to pay per month if you wanted to repay your mortgage in 20 years? How much interest would you save by paying off the mortgage in 20 rather than 30 years (go to the full table)?

A.

Exercise 15.5 Comparing Monthly Payments on Fixed and Adjustable Rate Loans

HSH Associates publishes the national averages for 30-year fixed and 1-year adjustable rate loans. Use these rates to calculate the monthly payment on a $100,000 30-year mortgage with the HSH Associates' Mortgage Calculator. Enter the average current contract rate on 30-year fixed-rate mortgages and 1-year adjustable-rate mortgages.

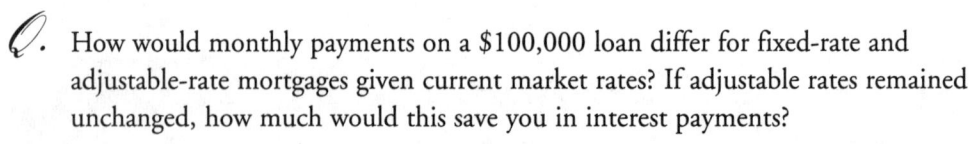

Q. How would monthly payments on a $100,000 loan differ for fixed-rate and adjustable-rate mortgages given current market rates? If adjustable rates remained unchanged, how much would this save you in interest payments?

A.

Exercise 15.6 Interest Savings on a Biweekly Mortgage

HSH Associates Mortgage Calculator can also be used to calculate the payoff on a biweekly mortgage.

Q. Given the 30-year fixed-rate mortgage you used in the previous exercise, how much sooner would you pay off this mortgage with biweekly payments? How much would you save in interest payments?

A.

Exercise 15.7 Calculating a Rate Adjustment

HSH Associates provides ARM Check Kit for calculating the rate change on a variable-rate mortgage. On the index histories page you can find recent information on the most popular ARM indexes.

Q. Which mortgage would have a lower contract rate: one using the weekly rate on the 10-year Treasury security with a two point margin, or one using the national mortgage contract interest rate with a one-point margin? The answer is likely to vary with the most recent economic conditions.

A.

Exercise 15.8 Comparing Future Payments Under Fixed-Rate and Adjustable-Rate Mortgages

This site from Belmont National Bank has several mortgage comparison calculators. The fixed-rate vs. adjustable-rate calculators are great for comparing the worst-case outcome for an adjustable-rate mortgage versus what would occur with a fixed-rate mortgage. Assuming maximum upward adjustments each period, it indicates at what point the fixed-rate mortgage becomes the optimal choice.

For example, the program indicates that given a 30-year fixed-rate mortgage at 8.75% and a 30-year annually adjusted mortgage with an initial rate of 4.75%, an annual cap of 2%, and a lifetime cap of 6%, the fixed rate would be more cost-effective by the end of the seventh year. This assumes that the ARM increases by the maximum each year and that other costs (fees and points) are comparable.

Q. How would the breakeven-year change if the fixed-rate mortgage had a 9.5% contract rate?

A.

Chapter 16
CONSUMER DURABLES
Satisfying Your Continuing Needs

CONSUMER DURABLES AND THE HOUSEHOLD BUDGET

Exercise 16.1 Calculating Price Changes

The Inflation Calculator from NASA allows you to calculate the percentage change in prices between any two years. It also provides a forecast of price changes for future years. You can calculate past price increases from 1913 to 1997 using the the Consumer Price Index (CPI) Inflation Calculator. For example, if you look at the price change between 1990 and 1995, you will see that the typical basket of consumer goods rose 16.6%.

The NASA site also contains a GDP Deflator Inflation Calculator. The GDP deflator is similar to the Consumer Price Index. However, it is based on a more inclusive market basket that includes non-consumer goods. Moreover, the fiscal year employed in this calculator is different from the calendar year in the Consumer Price Index (CPI) Inflation Calculator.

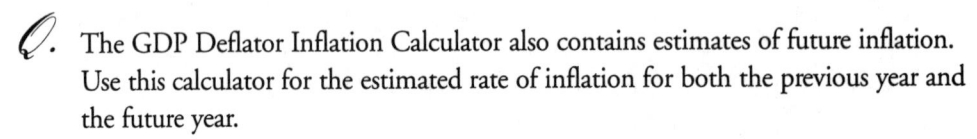

Q. The GDP Deflator Inflation Calculator also contains estimates of future inflation. Use this calculator for the estimated rate of inflation for both the previous year and the future year.

A.

SELECTING AN AUTOMOBILE

Exercise 16.2 Which Is Better: A New or Used Auto?

Go to the "New or Used Car?" calculator at the Finance Center. This calculator lets you compare the annual cost of depreciation and finance costs on a new car versus those on an old car. Compare the average annual cost of a new car and a one-year old car. You will no doubt be amazed at the cost difference. Be sure to go to the Average Cost Per Year ($) link. You will find a good explanation of the financial calculations and the time value of money. Don't overlook the other interesting calculators: auto loans versus home equity loans, rebate versus special dealer financing, and lease versus purchase.

Q. Using the same loan rate, what is the average cost per year on a $20,000 new car versus a 3-year-old used car?

A.

Exercise 16.3 How Much Is My Car Worth?

The Kelly Blue Book contains estimates on the market price of used cars. The website provides price estimates on both new and used cars. If contains price information on almost every make of car and every price option you can think of. Best of all, it is totally free.

Q. Select a make and model that hasn't changed much over the last 5 years, such as the Toyota Camry. Using today's pricing data from the Kelly Blue Book, estimate how a new car is likely to depreciate over the next 5 years? Assume you drive the car 20,000 miles a year and that you keep it in good condition.

A.

Exercise 16.4 Find the Monthly Cost of an Auto Lease

The AutoSite Loan/Lease Comparison Calculator at Cnet Central lets you compare the monthly payments on a purchase versus a lease.

Q. For the car of your choice, what is the monthly lease payment on a 24-month lease versus the monthly loan payment on a 24-month loan?

A.

WHAT IF YOU BOUGHT A LEMON ?

Exercise 16.5 Check Out Vehicle Recalls

Autosite has an online database that helps you track down manufacturer's recalls on most cars. Especially when safety-related recalls are necessary, manufacturers will try to locate present owners their vehicles. However, with a public that is always on the move, it is possible to lose track of owners of even recently purchased vehicles.

Q. Enter a make and model into the database. What are the outstanding recalls on this car? Are any of them safety-related?

A.

Exercise 16.6 Checking Out the BBB Autoline

The BBB Autoline Program helps manufactures and consumers resolve disputes through mediation and arbitration. Check to see if your car or your family's car is covered by this program. At this site you can also electronically file a complaint against a manufacturer. You can review the complaint form under "Request for BBB AUTO LINE Program Information." Be sure to check out the Lemon Car Page for lots of information on lemon programs across the country.

Q. What kinds of disputes are handled by BBB AUTO LINE?

A.

Exercise 16.7 Does Your State Have a Lemon Law?

This site at Cars.Com has information on state-specific lemon laws. You can find out whether your state has a law. If it does, you can get information on how the law is applied and under what conditions you may be entitled to full reimbursement.

Q. Is there a lemon law in your state? If so, what's covered and how is it applied?

A.

Chapter 17
RETIREMENT AND PENSION PLANNING
Planning for Your Long-Term Needs

SAVING AND INVESTING FOR RETIREMENT

Exercise 17.1 The Cost of Waiting

The Prudential Company has a calculator that demonstrates the power of tax deferral. Enter your monthly savings and your tax bracket, and it calculates how much more you would save at retirement by putting your funds in a tax-deferred account.

Q. Suppose you set aside $100 a month. How much will you have accumulated by retirement at age 65? Now suppose you delay the beginning of this savings plan for five years. How much less will you save by age 65 retirement?

A.

Exercise 17.2 Roth IRA or Traditional IRA?

The Roth IRA Calculator from Aetna lets you compare accumulations and after-tax disbursements from a Roth IRA and a traditional IRA. Depending on you current income and relative marginal tax bracket in your retirement years, one of these IRAs may be more favorable than the other.

Q. By assuming different marginal tax rates in the contribution and retirement years, provide an example in which the Roth IRA is the preferred investment vehicle. Now repeat your analysis, but this time provide an example in which the traditional IRA is the preferred investment vehicle.

A.

ESTABLISHING A PERSONAL RETIREMENT PLAN

Exercise 17.3 How Long Do You Need to Plan For?

The Insurance News Network provides life expectancy tables. Look up your life expectancy for your current age. Choose a retirement age and find the life expectancy for that retirement age.

Q. Can you explain why your current life expectancy differs from your life expectancy at retirement?

A.

Exercise 17.4 Selecting a Portfolio of Retirement Investments

How much you plan to save for retirement will depend on many factors. You have to consider your short-term needs, your present assets, and your attitude toward risk. The investor risk profiler from Regional Bank may give you some idea about which investments are right for you.

Q. How and why does the investment portfolio for the risk taker differ from the investment portfolio for the risk-adverse individual?

A.

Exercise 17.5 How Much Do You Need to Save for Retirement?

Fidelity Investments has one of the best retirement planning calculators on the world wide web. It allows you to control almost every variable that will affect how much you need to save today to satisfy tomorrow's retirement needs. It does all of the difficult calculations for you. You input expected inflation and earnings, but it automatically calculates annual inflation-adjusted requirements. If you can't link up with Fidelity, try the Vanguard Investments Retirement Calculator or the Torrid Technologies' Retirement Planner; they are both equally as good.

Enter values that reflect either your current economic status or what your economic status will be when you begin full-time employment. Be sure to note the assumptions you enter into the calculator. Estimate how much you would have to save each year in to fund what you consider a comfortable retirement.

Q. Change the retirement age from 65 to 55. How much more do you have to save each year to fund a comfortable early retirement?

A.

Exercise 17.6 How Much Income Will $100,000 Buy?

RetireWeb has its Retirement Annuity Calculator, which lets you estimate the present cost of a future retirement annuity. The cost will depend upon many factors. The major ones will be your present age and future retirement age, interest returns on the annuity accumulation, and the method of payout.

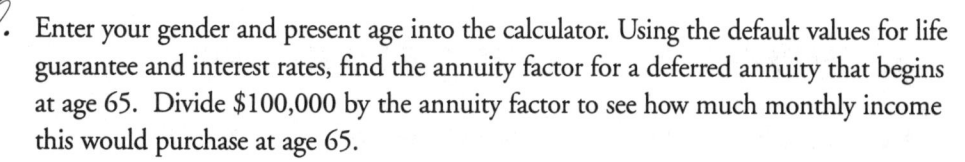

Q. Enter your gender and present age into the calculator. Using the default values for life guarantee and interest rates, find the annuity factor for a deferred annuity that begins at age 65. Divide $100,000 by the annuity factor to see how much monthly income this would purchase at age 65.

A.

Chapter 18
ESTATE PLANNING
Dividing up What's Left

TRANSFERRING YOUR ESTATE THROUGH A WILL

Exercise 18.1 Review the Wills of Famous People

Your will is a public document, which is open to the scrutiny of anyone who has an interest in examining your last words. Mark Welch's Wills on the Web has a large collection of wills from famous people. Court TV Wills of Notable People is also an interesting site. Elvis may no longer be with us, but his will is.

Q. Jerry Garcia's will indicates that all of his children were from previous marriages. How does he ensure that these children will receive a fair share of the estate?

A.

DEATH TAXES, AND OTHER RELATED TAX ISSUES

Exercise 18.2 Calculate the Federal Tax on the Taxable Estate

On a large estate the federal estate taxes can take a large bite out of what you may leave your beneficiaries. ITT Hartford's Estate Tax Calculator is an easy way of finding the estate tax liability.

Q. Vary the taxable estate from $1 million to $2 million. How does the estate tax change, and what is the marginal tax rate on the second million?

A.

Exercise 18.3 Recent Changes in Estate Tax Law

Hall and Dorr, a California law firm, publishes annual updates covering recent changes in the law. The Hale & Dorr Trusts & Estates Bulletin contains the annual highlights for tax and estate law modifications.

Q. Summarize one of the changes highlighted in the most recent bulletin.

A.

Internet Addresses

Internet addresses are in a constant state of change. Imagine what it would be like if every time you got on the interstate highway it took a new route. It still heads in the general direction you want to go, but it doesn't pass through the same towns and the exits may have been moved. That's what it is like when you travel the Internet. You are likely to discover that several of the following addresses may have been changed or are no longer functioning. Don't worry; you can find an updated road map at **http://www.prenhall.com/winger**. This site contains the latest links for the previous exercises. It also links to many other useful resources on personal financial planning. Rather than directly entering these addresses into your browser, we suggest you first visit our book site.

Aetna	www.aetna.com/aeindex.htm
American Hospital Directory	www.ahd.com/guestLGL.html
American Numismatic Association	www.money.org
ARM Check Kit	www.hsh.com
Autosite	www.autosite.com
AutoSite Loan/Lease Comparison Calculator	www.search.com/Single/0,7,400503,00.html
Bank Rate Monitor	www.bankrate.com
BBB Autoline Program	www.bbb.org
Belmont National Bank	www.belmontbank.com
BLS Consumer Expenditure Survey	stats.bls.gov
Bonds On-Line	www.bonds-online.com
Bureau of Labor Statistics	stats.bls.gov
California Health Care Shopper	www.healthcareshopper.com
Cars.Com	cartalk.cars.com
CBS MarketWatch	cbs.marketwatch.com/news/newsroom.htx
Census Bureau	www.census.gov
Centura Money Managers	www.centura.com
Checkfree Corporation	www.checkfree.com
Chicago Board of Trade	www.cbot.com
Cnet Central,	www.search.com
Coldwell Banker	www.coldwellbanker.com
Commercial Union Life	www.culife.com
Consumer Guide to Advance Directives	www.ghc.org/health_info/adv_dir/advpage.html
cost of homeowner's insurance	www.insure.com
Court TV Wills of Notable People	www.courttv.com/legaldocs/newsmakers/wills
CUNA & Affiliates	www.cuna.org
DBC Online	www.dbc.com
Deloitte & Touche OnLine	www.dtonline.com
Dogs of the Dow	dogsofthedow.com
EagleWing Research	www.eaglewing.com
Economic Statistics Briefing Room	www.whitehouse.gov/fsbr/esbr.html
Economics Time Series Page	bos.business.uab.edu
Equifax	www.equifax.com
Estate Tax Calculator	www.thehartford.com
E-Trade	www.etrade.com
Federal Reserve Bank of New York	www.ny.frb.org
Federal Tax Administrators	www.taxadmin.org
Federation of Tax Administrators,	www.taxadmin.org/fta/rate/ind_inc.html
Fidelity Investment Center	www.fid-inv.com
Finance Center	www.financenter.com
Hall and Dorr,	www.haledorr.com
HealthCash	www.healthy.net/library/articles/cash/assessment/assessment.htm
Highway Loss Data Institute	www.carsafety.org
Household Budget Management	dacomp.hypermart.net
HSH Associates	www.hsh.com

Hugh Chou	www.interest.com/hugh/calc
ICI	www.ici.org
Inflation Calculator from NASA	www.jsc.nasa.gov/bu2/inflate.html
Insurance Information News	www.insure.com/states/index.html
Insurance News Network	www.insure.com/ratings/index.html
IntelliQuote	146.145.38.124/cgi-win/wrqver10.exe/158
Internal Revenue Service	www.irs.ustreas.gov/prod
Joint Commission on Accreditation of Healthcare Organizations	wwwa.jcaho.org/directry
Kelly Blue Book	www.kbb.com
KeyPartners	www.underwriter.com
Lemon Car Page	www.mindspring.com
Life and Health Insurance Foundation for Education	www.life-line.org
Martindale's 'The Reference Desk'	www-sci.lib.uci.edu/HSG/RefCalculators.html
Money Advisor	www.timevalue.com/mapval.htm
Money Advisor,	www.moneyadvisor.com/calc
Money Online	cgi.pathfinder.com/cgi-bin/Money/instant.cgi
Morningstar Fund Reports	www.investools.com/cgi-bin/Library/msmf.pl
Mortgage Calculator	www.interest.com/monthly-payment.html
Mutual Funds Interactive	www.brill.com
NASDAQ	www.nasdaq.com
National Association of Enrolled Agents	www.naea.org
National Association of Investment Clubs	www.better-investing.org
Netstock Direct	www.netstockdirect.com
Network Payment Mechanisms	ganges.cs.tcd.ie/mepeirce/project.html
New York Stock Exchange	www.nyse.com
Northwestern Mutual Life's online life expectancy calculator	www.northwesternmutual.com/games/longevity
Online Money	pathfinder.com/@@b0i@tgYAuI9WJL7a/money/intuit/features/auditbait_0196/index.html
Prudential Company	www.prudential.com
Prudential Securities	www.prusec.com
QuickQuote	www.quickquote.com
Quotesmith	www.quotesmith.com
Regatta QRetire in Style	www.regattaq.com/r3.html
Regional Bank	www.regionalbank.com
RetireWeb	www.retireweb.com
Rio Grande Free-Net	rgfn3.epcc.edu/health/index.html
Securities and Exchange Commission (SEC)	www.sec.gov
Securities and Exchange Commission (SEC)	www.sec.gov/edaux/formlynx.htm
Security APL, Inc.	qs.secapl.com
Smith/Barney	www.smithbarney.com
Social Security Online	www.ssa.gov
Social Security Statistical Tables	www.ssa.gov/OACT/STATS/statTab.html
St. Louis Federal Reserve Bank	www.stls.frb.org/fred/data/iupdate.html
Standard and Poors ratings	data.insure.com/ratings
Stockmaster	www.stockmaster.com
Tax Sites State Government Tax List	www.best.com/~ftmexpat/html/taxsites/statelaw.html
The Best Price Guide	beaniebabies.thebestguide.com
The Card You Pick Can Save You Money."	www.pueblo.gsa.gov/cic_text/money/shop/shop.html
The National Association of Real Estate Investment Trusts	www.nareit.com
The National Committee on Quality Assurance	www.ncqa.org/Pages/Main/index.htm
TIGER Map Service	tiger.census.gov
Time Share Users Group	www.tug2.net
Trans Union,	www.tuc.com
TRW (Experian),	www.experian.com
Ty Company	www.ty.com
Unknown Loan Variables Calculator from Bank 2000	www.bank2000.com
USA Today	usatoday.com
Values and Lifestyles Program (VALS) at SRI	http://future.sri.com/VALS/survey.html
Vanguard	www.vanguard.com/educ/lib/library.html
Wills on the Web	www.ca-probate.com/wills.htm
WSRN.com	www.wsrn.com
Yahoo Quotes	quote.yahoo.com